Piss Off

Hilarious Sweary Coloring Book for Fun & Stress Relief

By

S.B. Nozaz

Copyright © 2016 by S.B. Nozaz

All rights reserved worldwide. No part of this publication may be reproduced or distributed in any form or by any means, mechanical, electronic or stored in a retrieval or database system, without written permission from the copyright holder.

FUCKERPALOOZA

OLD FART

CALM YOUR TITS

MOTHERFUCKER

DAMN YOU

EAT SHIT

DAMN

YOU ARE

SHIT

OUT OF LUCK

SHIT BRAIN

WHAT A PUSSY

JERK

ASSHOLE

Note

www.ingramcontent.com/pod-product-compliance
Lightning Source LLC
Chambersburg PA
CBHW080635190526
45169CB00009B/3402